Dedicated
to the memory of
Mirko Hanak
who brought so much beauty
to children everywhere

Copyright © 1972 by Scroll Press, Inc.
22 East 84th St., New York, N.Y. 10028
Library of Congress No. 72-89571
All rights reserved
Printed in the United States of America

ANIMALS WE LOVE

by Mirko Hanak

Book 1

Scroll Press, New York

Look around, and you see animals everywhere.
  In the country.
  In cities.
  On farms.
  In the sky.
  In trees.
  And under the water.
Some are wild, and some belong to people.

Let's learn about some of these animals.
  About where they live.
  About what they do.
  About what they look like.
  And about what they eat.
Let's read this book and find out!

Squirrels live high in trees.
They run along the branches and make nests
  out of leaves and twigs.
During the summer, squirrels find many nuts
  and acorns to eat, and they grow fat.
But in the fall they must hide nuts so they
  will have food during the winter.

Some squirrels are as tiny as mice.
Others are as big as cats.
Some are red.
Some are black.
And some are brown.
Some squirrels have flaps of skin between
    their front and back legs that are like wings.
These flying squirrels can glide through the air
    from tree to tree.

Otters live in streams and marshes where
they catch fish for their families.
They have long, thick fur that keeps them
warm when they get wet.
And they have shiny black eyes that see
danger quickly.

To keep their families safe, otters build
their homes in a hole in the river bank.
The door is hidden under the water so
enemies cannot find it.

Otters are full of fun.
They like to jump and splash in the water.
They make slides in slippery grass or snow
   and slither down river banks into the water.
They have fun playing with each other!

porcupine is not very cuddly!
Except for his tummy and parts of his face
  he is covered with sharp, prickly quills.
Porcupines live in forests where they build
  their homes in hollow trees.
They sleep during the day, and go out at night
  to look for plants and tree bark to eat.

Porcupines may look dangerous, but they are
  not fierce at all.
They use their quills only when an enemy attacks.
Then they whirl around with their back to the
  enemy and stand their quills on end.
Porcupines cannot throw their quills, but if the
  enemy touches them, the quills stick into him.
And he won't bother a porcupine again!

Owls sleep during the day and wake up at night
   to hunt for food.
Because they are awake when it is dark, they
   have large eyes to help them see better.
They have better hearing than any other bird.
This helps them hear small animals when they
   are hunting in the dark.

Owls build their nests in many places.
   In tree hollows.
   Or in deserted woodpecker nests.
   Or in barns or steeples.
   Or in burrows dug by other animals.

Many people think owls are very wise.
But compared with other birds they are neither
   the most wise nor the most stupid.

Llamas live high in the mountains in South America.
They have sharp little hoofs that grip the steep
    rocks and help them climb easily.
Like their relatives—the camels—llamas can
    travel very far without drinking water.
And they are very strong and can carry heavy loads.

Therefore llamas are very valuable in South America.
People use llamas to carry their heavy loads over
    the high mountain trails.
And they use the llama's long hair to make warm
    clothes to protect them from the mountain winds.

But llamas have one bad habit
 people don't like.
When they are mad—they spit!

Foxes are related to dogs.
They look like dogs with long red fur, sharp
   muzzels, and big bushy tails.
The fox family builds its home in a hole
   in the ground.

The pups are born in a warm nest in this burrow.
Four to six fox pups are born each spring.
When they are born, they are blind.
They cannot see anything for almost two weeks.
But as they grow bigger, they are allowed to go
   out of the burrow to play.

While the pups play around the burrow, their
  parents go out hunting for dinner.
Foxes are good parents.
Both the mother and father work hard to take
  care of their pups and bring them food.
Foxes do most of their hunting at night.
They go out quietly to search for small
  animals and birds.

Because foxes are very clever and sly, they
    make very good hunters.
The biggest enemies that foxes have are
    the people who hunt them for their fur.
But foxes are very smart, and they often
    outwit men and avoid the traps they set.

Some swans are wild and live deep in
   the country.
Others are tame and live in parks or zoos.

When they are grownup, they are pure white
   with long graceful necks.
They use their long necks to reach far down
   into the water to eat water plants.

Swans build big nests with twigs, grass,
   and leaves on the ground near the water.
In the spring the mother swan lays three
   to six eggs.
She takes good care of the eggs.
If she has to leave them, she covers them
   with a blanket of moss.

In June the babies hatch.
They are called cygnets.
They have ash gray feathers, and they do not
 turn pure white until they are two years old.

Rabbits live all over the world.
They have strong back legs for jumping and
    smaller front legs for running and balancing.
They have short fluffy tails, long wiggly ears,
    and long sharp front teeth for nibbling.

Because of their powerful back legs, rabbits
    can hop very fast.
Some jack rabbits can hop at thirty miles an hour
    and can jump ten feet in one leap.

Rabbits eat grass, vegetables, and grain.
They especially like a farmer's garden.
That is why farmers do not like them!

When baby rabbits are born,
   they are blind.
They have no fur at all.
The mother rabbit builds
   a nest lined with fur.
The babies live in it
   for two weeks
   before they can see.

Some rabbits are brown and some are black.
Some tame ones are white with pink eyes.
Some animals that look like rabbits are
   really hares.

The snowshoe hare changes color during the year.
In the summer he is brown so his enemies cannot
   see him hidden on the ground.
But in winter, when the snow falls, his fur becomes
   white so he will be safe in the snow.
The fur on his paws becomes longer, making his paws
   like snowshoes so he can run on the snow easily.
That is why he got his name—the snowshoe hare.

There are many different kinds of bears.
   There are small brown bears.
   There are big white polar bears.
   And there are giant grizzly bears.

Most bears sleep during the day and wake up
   at night to eat and explore.
Bears eat some meat, but mainly they like nuts,
   fruit, honey, roots, grasses and insects.
Bears dig dens in the ground to live in.
   Or use dark caves.
   Or hollow trees.
   Or thickets made of branches and bushes.

Bears who live in cold places go to sleep
   for most of the winter in their dens.
Sometimes they wake up for a little while and
   sleepily eat some food.
In the early spring while the mother is still
   asleep, the cubs are born.

Most people think bears are very fierce.
Some are.
But usually they are more afraid of people
     than people are of them.
Usually they will not attack people unless
     they are bothered.

The pheasant is one of the most beautiful
  birds in the world.
It has a lovely long tail and bright feathers.
Pheasants live in many countries, but most
  people think they originally came from China.
They like to live near the edge of the forest
  on ground with thick undergrowth.
They come into the clearings and meadows to
  look for food.
Pheasants eat fruit, berries, seeds, grain,
  and sometimes insects.

When spring comes, pheasants build nests on
  the ground and lay eight to ten eggs.
The babies hatch out, and their parents bring
  them food until they are grown.

Deer live in most places around the world.
There are about fifty different kinds.
Some are as small as a little dog.
Some are as big as a large horse.

Usually deer are brown in color.
In winter their coat is heavy to keep them warm.
In summer it becomes light to keep them cool.

Deer eat grass, leaves, moss, bark, and buds.
They usually go out at night to search for food.
In winter it is hard to find grass to eat
   through the heavy snow.
Then deer strip the bark off the trees and
   eat it when they are hungry.

In the spring the mother deer goes to her
   thicket made of bushes deep in the forest.
There her fawns are born.
Sometimes there is one fawn.
Sometimes twins are born.

When they are born, they have white spots
   on their back.
These help protect them from enemies.
They make the fawn's back look like sunlight
   patterns on the ground.
When fawns are born, they have long thin legs.
At first they cannot walk.
But soon they struggle up on their wobbly legs
   and walk a little.
In a few days they can run, jump, and play
   in their thicket.

But their mother always makes sure that
   they stay near her.
That way they will be safe from enemies.